DRAW 50

SHARKS,

WHALES, AND OTHER SEA CREATURES

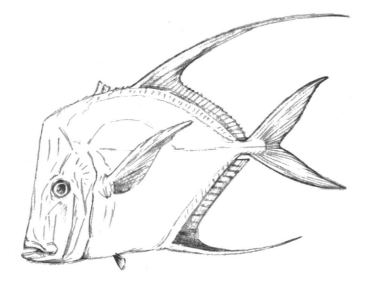

ALSO BY LEE J. AMES

Draw 50 Airplanes, Aircraft, and Spacecraft
Draw 50 Animals
Draw 50 Athletes
Draw 50 Beasties and Yugglies and Turnover Uglies and
      Things That Go Bump in the Night
Draw 50 Boats, Ships, Trucks, and Trains
Draw 50 Buildings and Other Structures
Draw 50 Cars, Trucks, and Motorcycles
Draw 50 Cats
Draw 50 Dinosaurs and Other Prehistoric Animals
Draw 50 Dogs
Draw 50 Famous Cartoons
Draw 50 Famous Faces
Draw 50 Famous Stars
Draw 50 Holiday Decorations
Draw 50 Horses
Draw 50 Monsters, Creeps, Superheroes, Demons, Dragons,
      Nerds, Dirts, Ghouls, Giants, Vampires, Zombies,
      and Other Curiosa . . .
Draw 50 Vehicles

DRAW 50
SHARKS,
WHALES, AND OTHER SEA CREATURES

LEE J. AMES
with Warren Budd

DOUBLEDAY
NEW YORK LONDON TORONTO SYDNEY AUCKLAND

Published by Doubleday, a division of
Bantam Doubleday Dell Publishing Group, Inc.,
666 Fifth Avenue, New York, New York 10103

Doubleday and the portrayal of an anchor with a dolphin
are trademarks of Doubleday, a division of
Bantam Doubleday Dell Publishing Group, Inc.

Library of Congress Cataloging-in-Publication Data
Ames, Lee J.
   Draw 50 sharks, whales, and other sea creatures / Lee J. Ames with
Warren Budd.—1st ed.
         p.   cm.
   Summary: Provides step-by-step instructions for drawing a variety
of sharks, whales, and other sea creatures, including the hammerhead
shark, humpback whale, and giant sea turtle.
   1. Sharks in art—Juvenile literature.   2. Whales in art—Juvenile
literature.   3. Marine fauna in art—Juvenile literature.
4. Drawing—Technique—Juvenile literature.   [1. Sharks in art.
2. Whales in art.   3. Marine animals in art.   4. Drawing—
Technique.]   I. Budd, Warren.   II. Title.   III. Title: Draw
fifty sharks, whales, and other sea creatures.
NC781.A44 1989
743'.6—dc19   88-35163
CIP
AC
ISBN: 0-385-24627-7
ISBN: 0-385-24628-5 (lib. bdg.)
Copyright © 1989 by Lee J. Ames and Murray D. Zak

To Warren, with great appreciation
for the wonderful job that you've done,
and there's nothing fishy about that remark.
L.J.A.

To Lee,
with thanks for the opportunity.
W.B.

TO THE READER

Perhaps by now you have come across one of my "Draw 50" books, or perhaps this is the first one you've ever picked up. Either way, I hope to show you in this book how to draw a wide variety of fascinating sea creatures. I have a great love and respect for the other creatures of this earth and for that reason, I've chosen to go underwater and give you a sampling of the wonderful life-forms that live there.

At first glance, the drawings in this book may appear difficult. But if you take your time and carefully follow the step-by-step instructions for each illustration, you will be able to produce a satisfying finished drawing.

To begin, you will need only clean paper, a pencil with moderately soft lead (HB or No. 2), and a kneaded eraser (available at art supply stores). Select the illustration you want to draw, and then *very lightly and carefully*, sketch out step number one. Then, also very *lightly and carefully*, add step number two to step number one. These steps, which may look the easiest, are the most important. A mistake here can ruin your entire drawing at the end. And remember to watch not only the lines themselves, but the *spaces between the lines* to make sure that they are the same as for the drawing in the book. As you sketch out these first steps, it might be a good idea to hold your work up to a mirror. Sometimes the mirror shows that you've twisted the drawing off to one side without being aware of it.

In each drawing, the new step is shown darker than the previous one so that it can be clearly seen. But you should keep your own work very light. Here's where the kneaded eraser will come in handy; use it to lighten your work after each step.

When you have finished your picture, you may want to go over it with some India ink. Apply this with a fine brush or pen. When the ink has thoroughly dried, erase the entire drawing with the kneaded eraser. The erasing will not affect the India ink.

The most important thing to remember is that even if your first attempts are not as good as you would like them to be, you should not get discouraged. Like any other talent, whether it be performing gymnastic feats or playing the piano, drawing takes practice to do your best.

Though there are many ways to learn how to draw, the step-by-step method used in this book should start you off in the right direction.

LEE J. AMES

TO THE PARENT
OR TEACHER

"Leslie can draw the best Great White Shark I ever saw!" Such peer acclaim and encouragement generate incentive. Contemporary methods of art instruction (freedom of expression, experimentation, self-evaluation of competence and growth) provide a vigorous, fresh-air approach for which we must all be grateful.

New ideas need not, however, totally exclude the old. One such is the "follow me, step-by-step" approach. In my young learning days this method was so common, and frequently so exclusive, that the student became nothing more than a pantographic extension of the teacher. In those days it was excessively overworked.

This does not mean that the young hand is never to be guided. Rather, specific guiding is fundamental. Step-by-step guiding that produces satisfactory results is valuable even when the means of accomplishment are not fully understood by the student.

The novice with a musical instrument is frequently taught to play simple melodies as quickly as possible, well before he or she learns the most elemental scratchings at the surface of music theory. The resultant self-satisfaction, pride in accomplishment, can provide significant motivation. And all from mimicking an instructor's "Do-as-I-do . . ."

Mimicry is prerequisite for developing creativity. We learn the use of our tools by mimicry. Then we can use those tools for creativity. To this end I would offer the budding artist the opportunity to memorize or mimic (rote-like, if you wish) the making of "pictures"—"pictures" he or she has been anxious to be able to draw.

The use of this book should be available to anyone who *wants* to try another way of flapping his or her wings. Perhaps he or she will then get off the ground when a friend says, "Leslie can draw the best Great White Shark I ever saw!"

LEE J. AMES

BLUE SHARK
Up to ten feet long

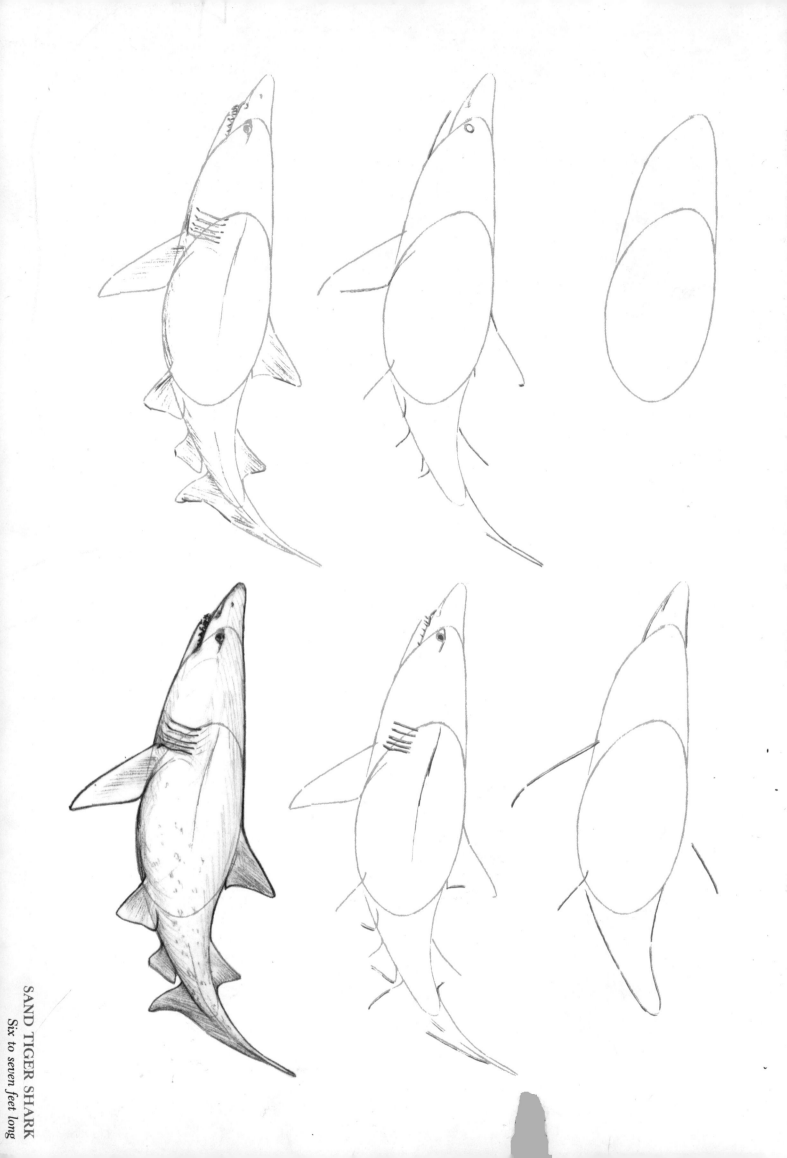

MAKO SHARK
Up to fifteen feet long

PACIFIC ANGEL SHARK
Up to five feet long

WHALE SHARK
Up to sixty feet long

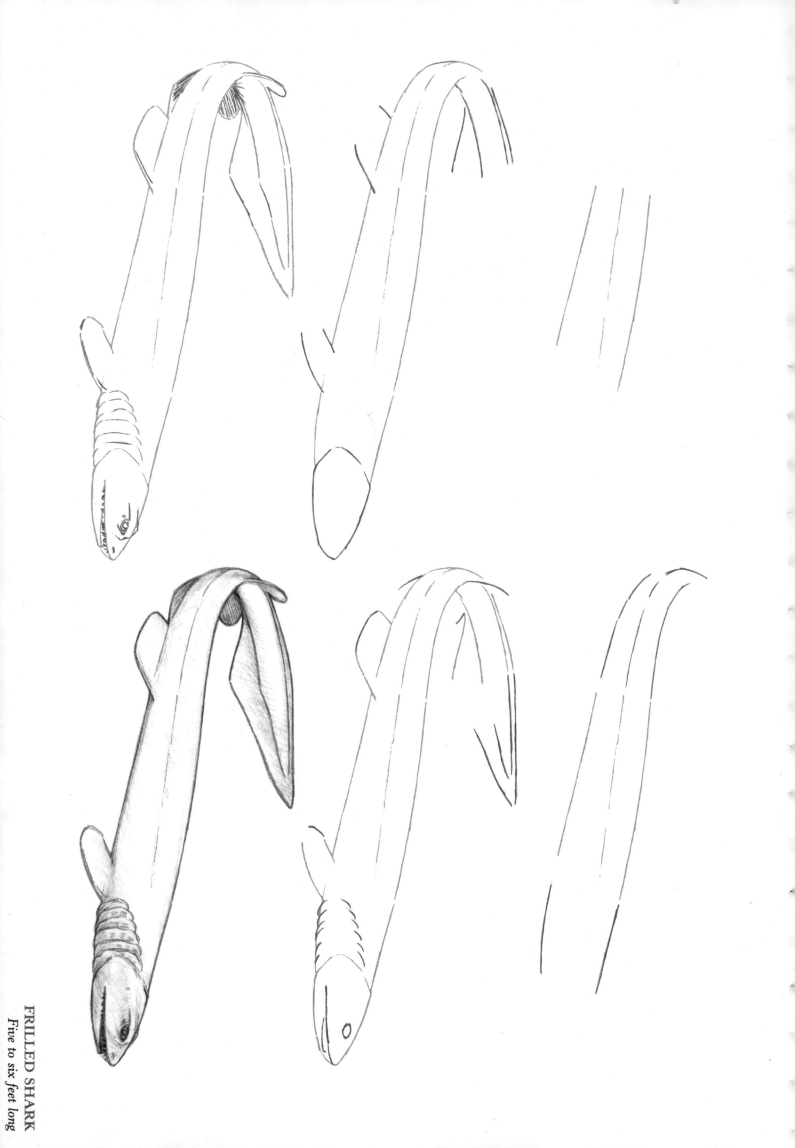

FRILLED SHARK

Five to six feet long

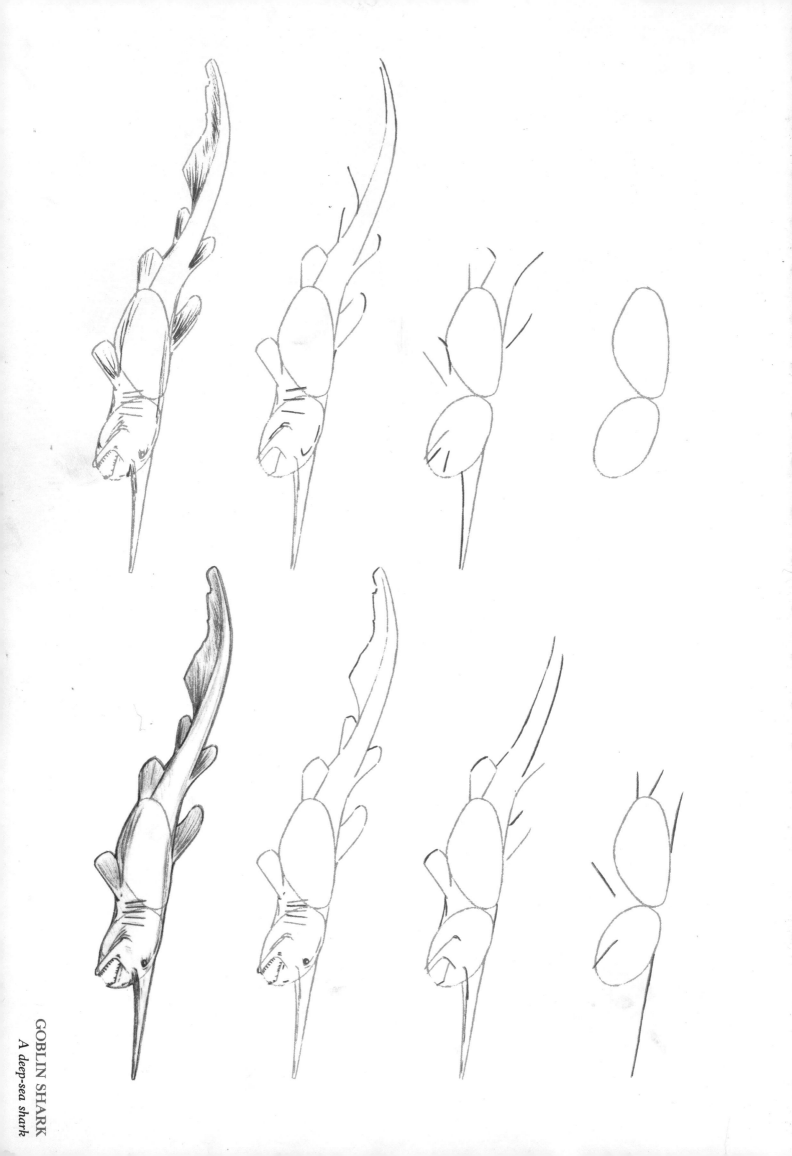

GOBLIN SHARK
A deep-sea shark

NURSE SHARK
Up to fourteen feet long

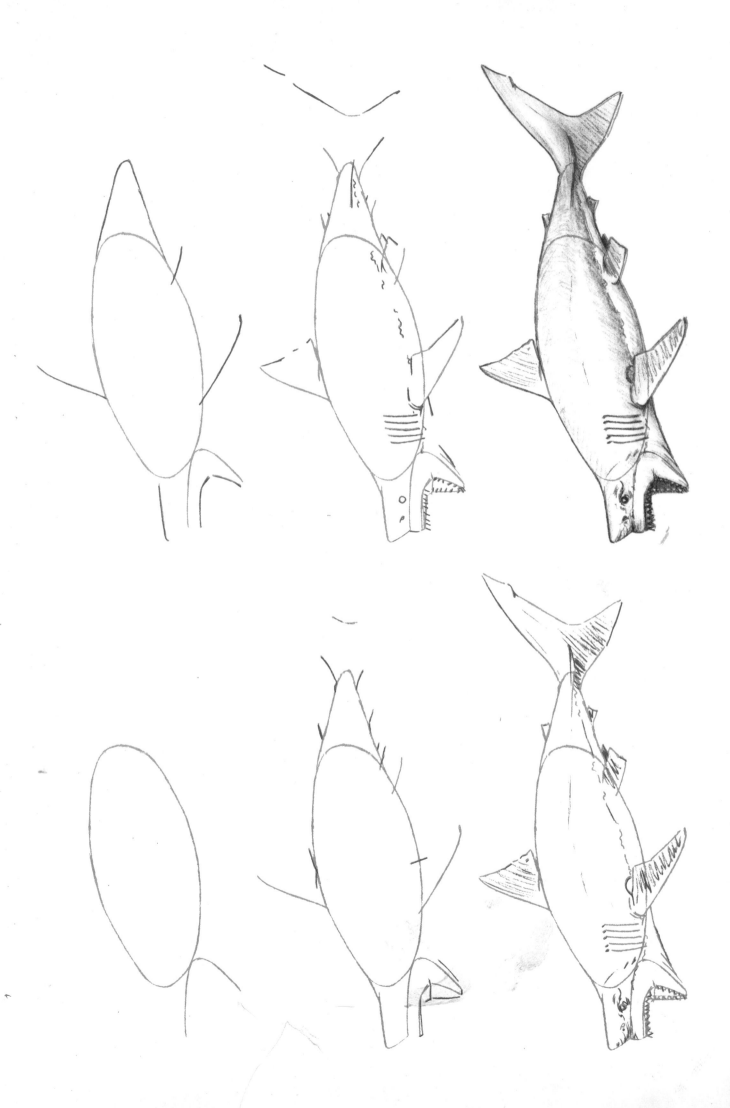

GREAT WHITE SHARK
Up to twenty-five feet long

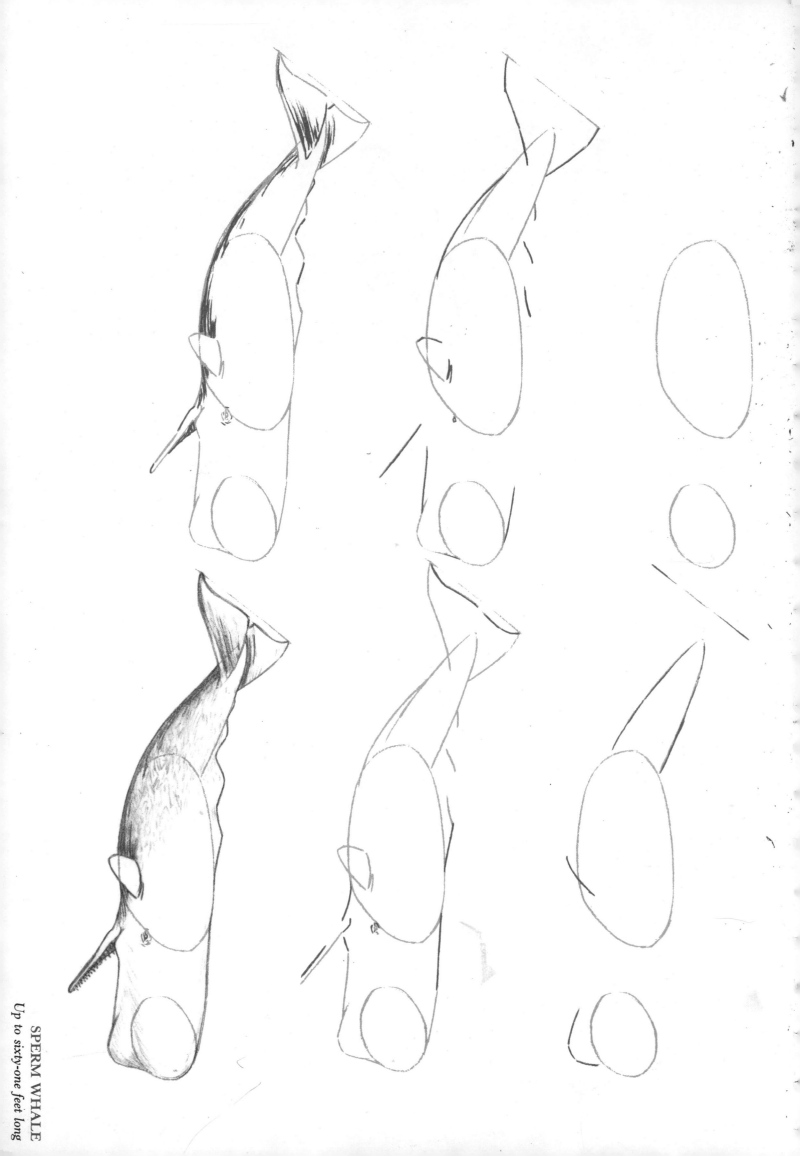

SPERM WHALE
Up to sixty-one feet long

KILLER WHALE
Up to thirty feet long

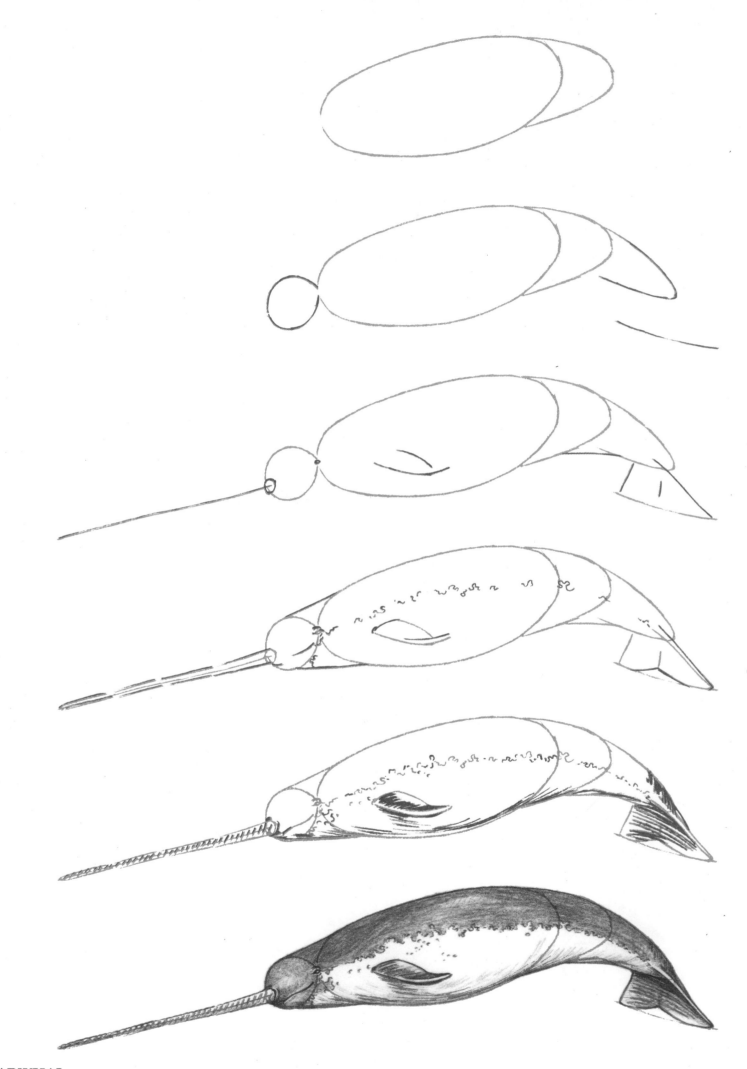

NARWHAL
Body is up to fifteen feet long.
The horn on some males grows to nine feet.

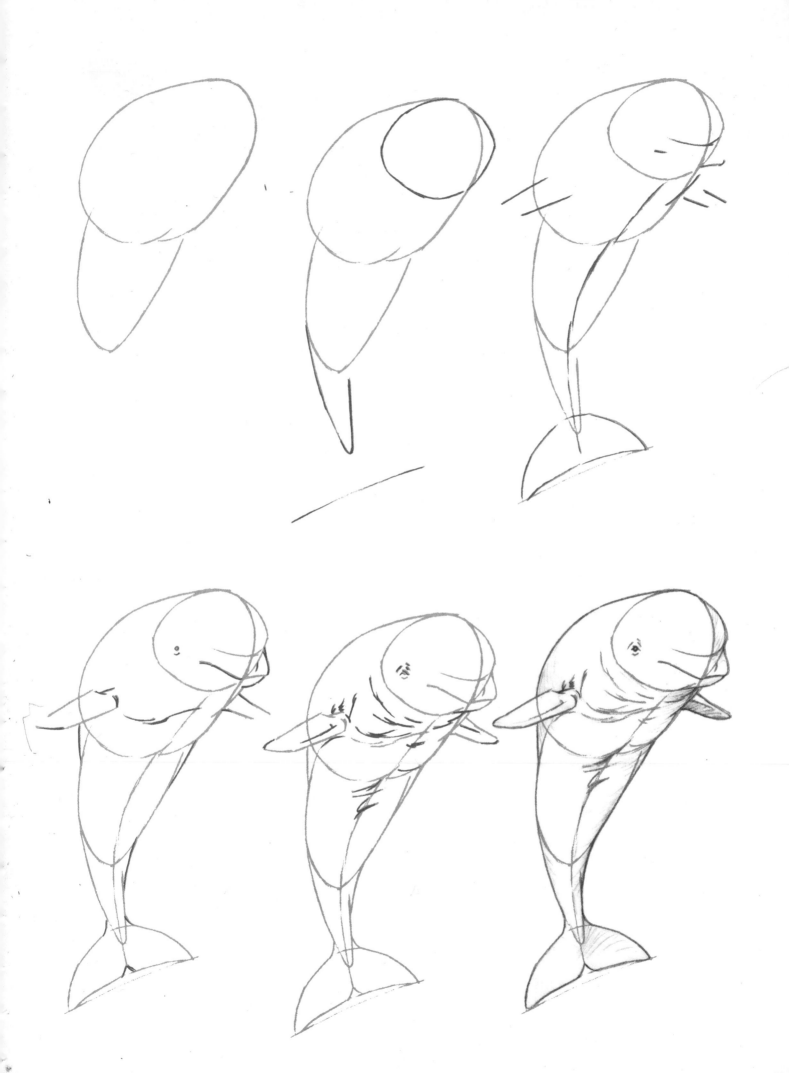

WHITE (BELUGA) WHALE
Up to twenty feet long

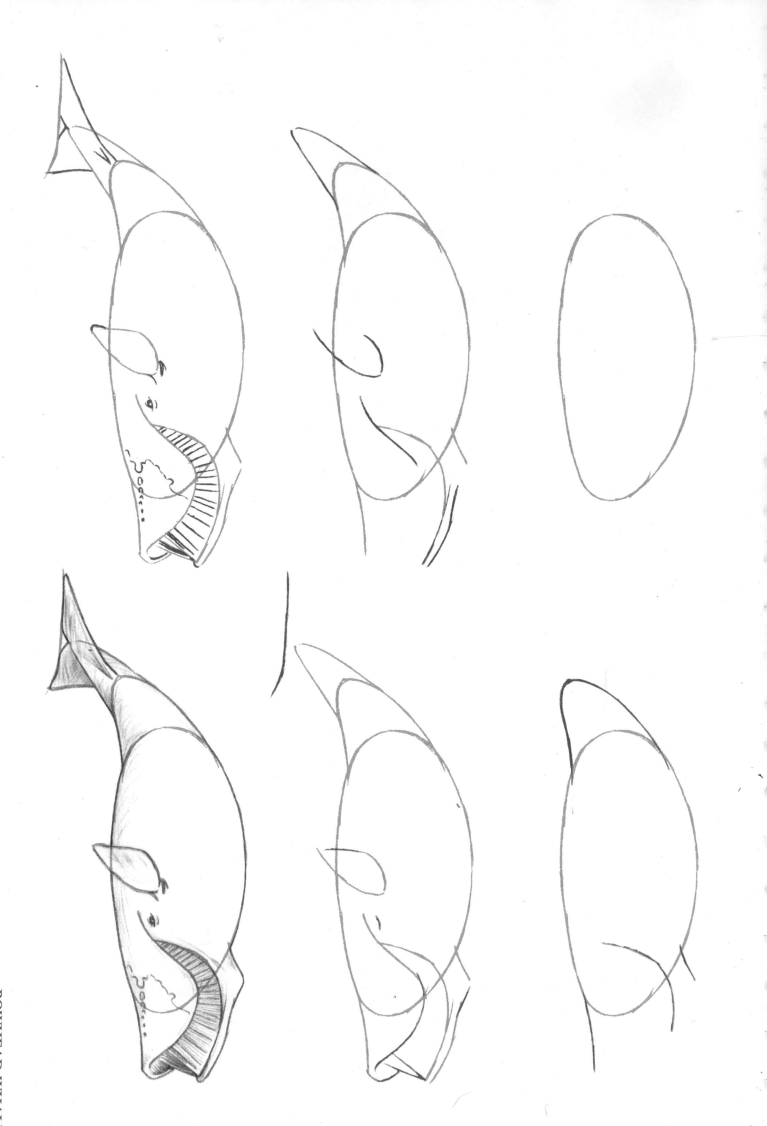

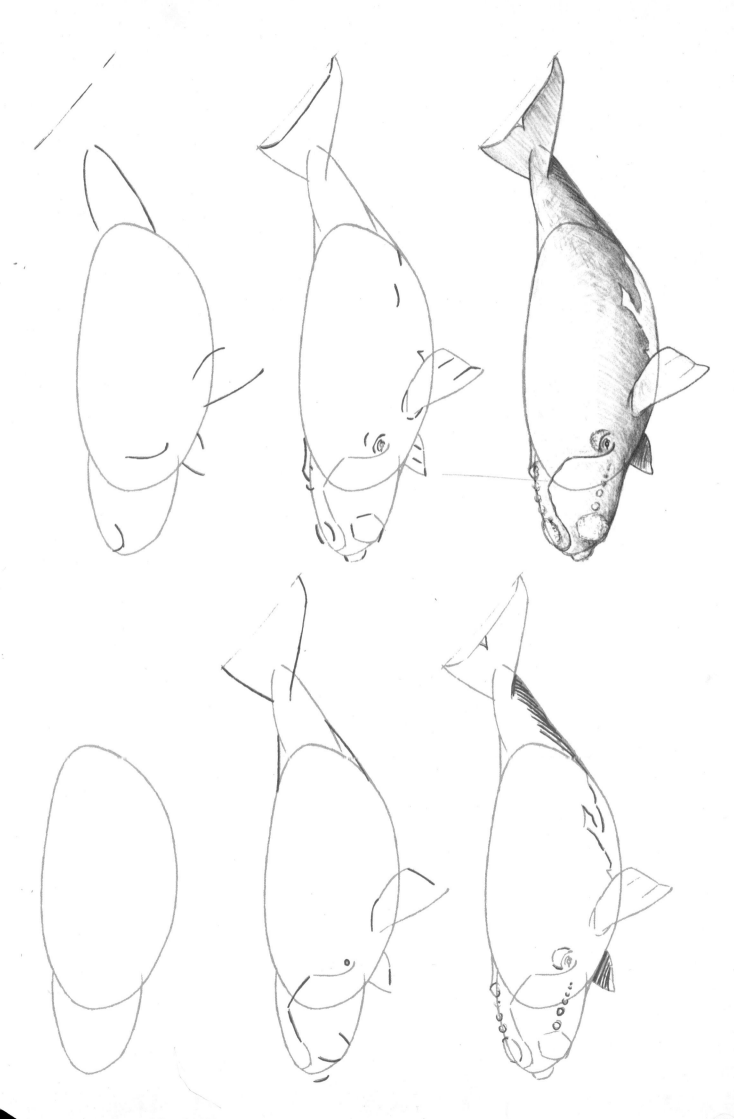

RIGHT WHALE
Up to sixty feet long

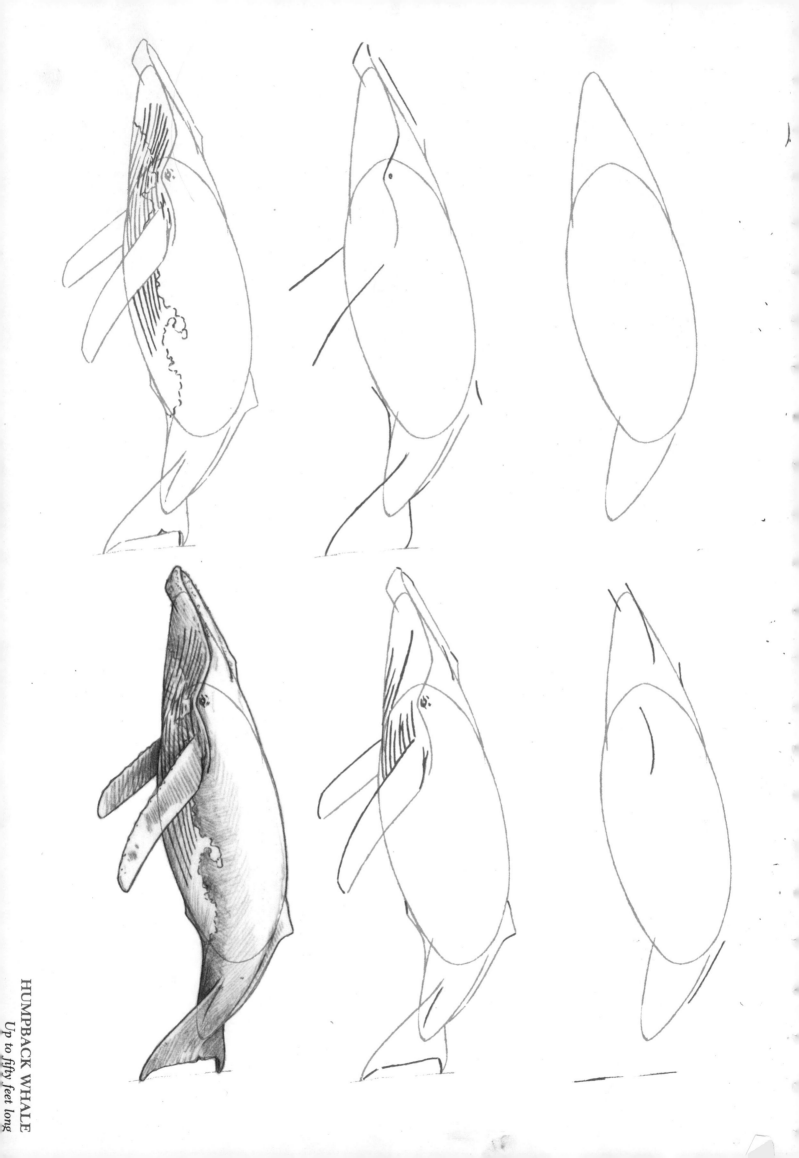

GRAY WHALE
Up to forty-five feet long

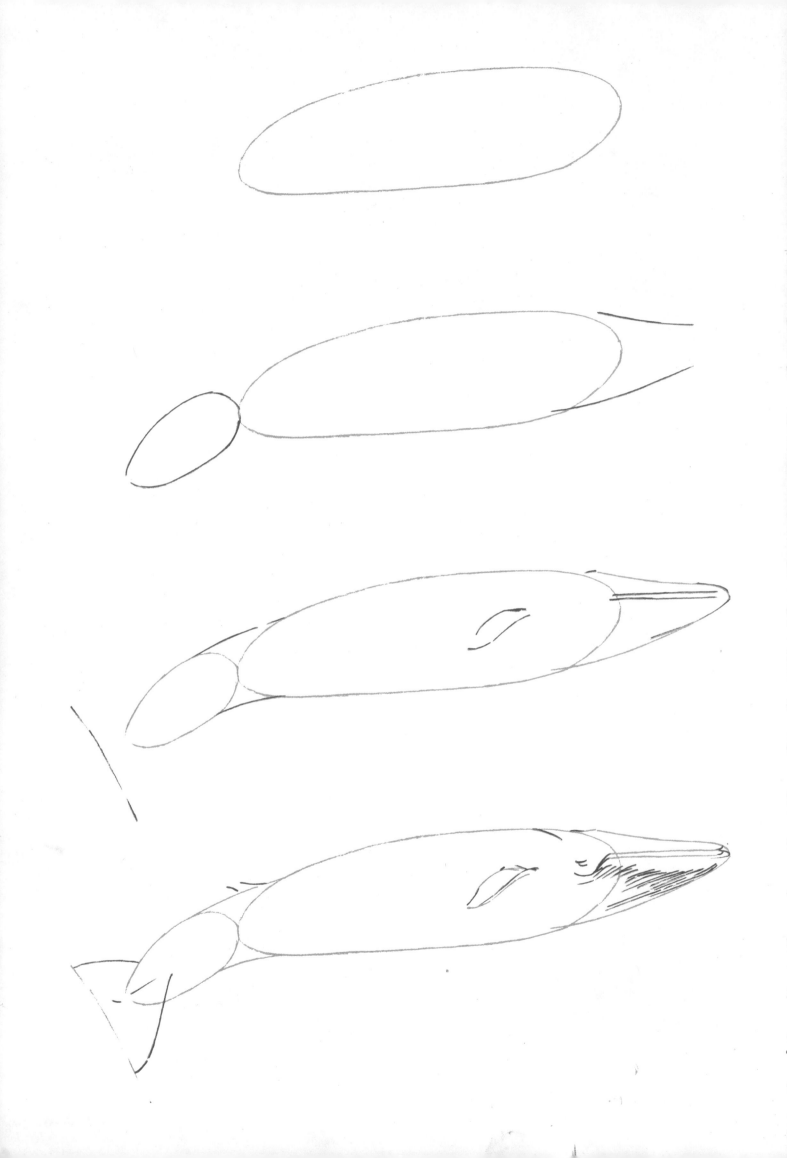

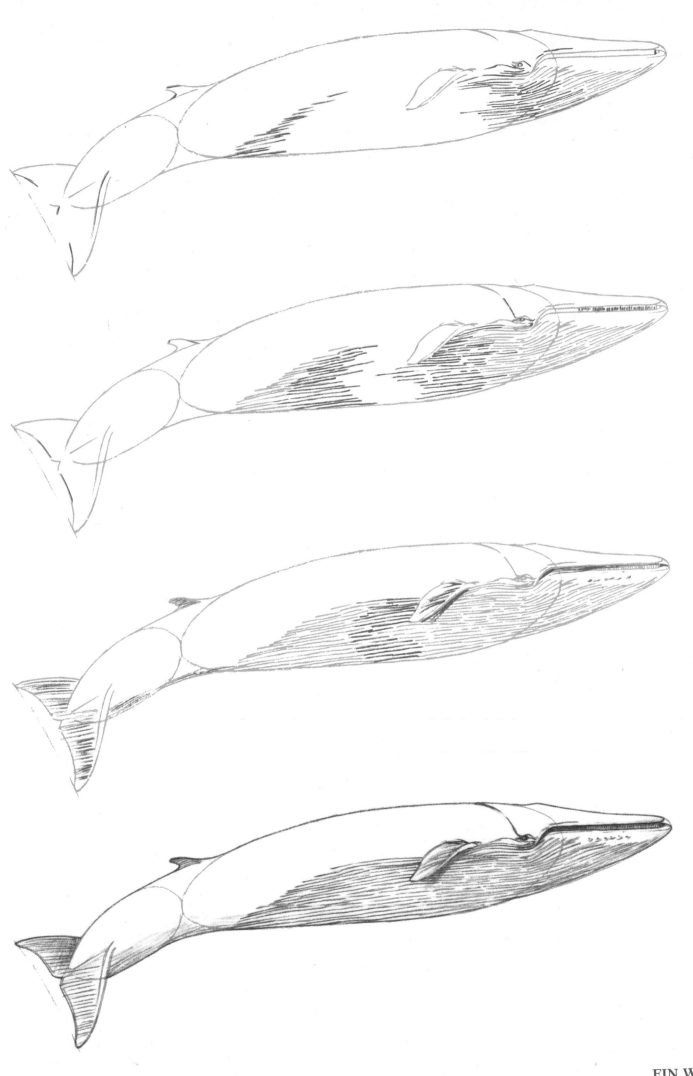

FIN WHALE
Up to eighty feet long

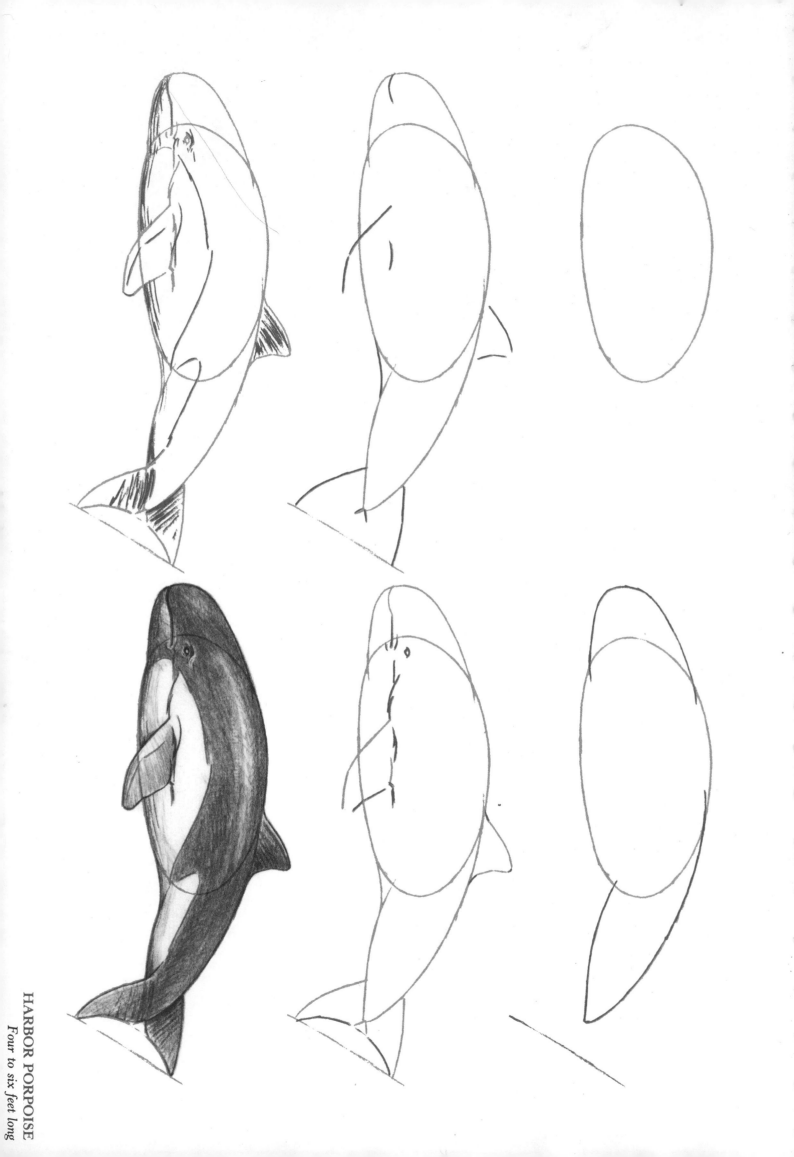

HARBOR PORPOISE
Four to six feet long

FALSE KILLER WHALE
Up to twenty feet long.
Belongs to dolphin family.

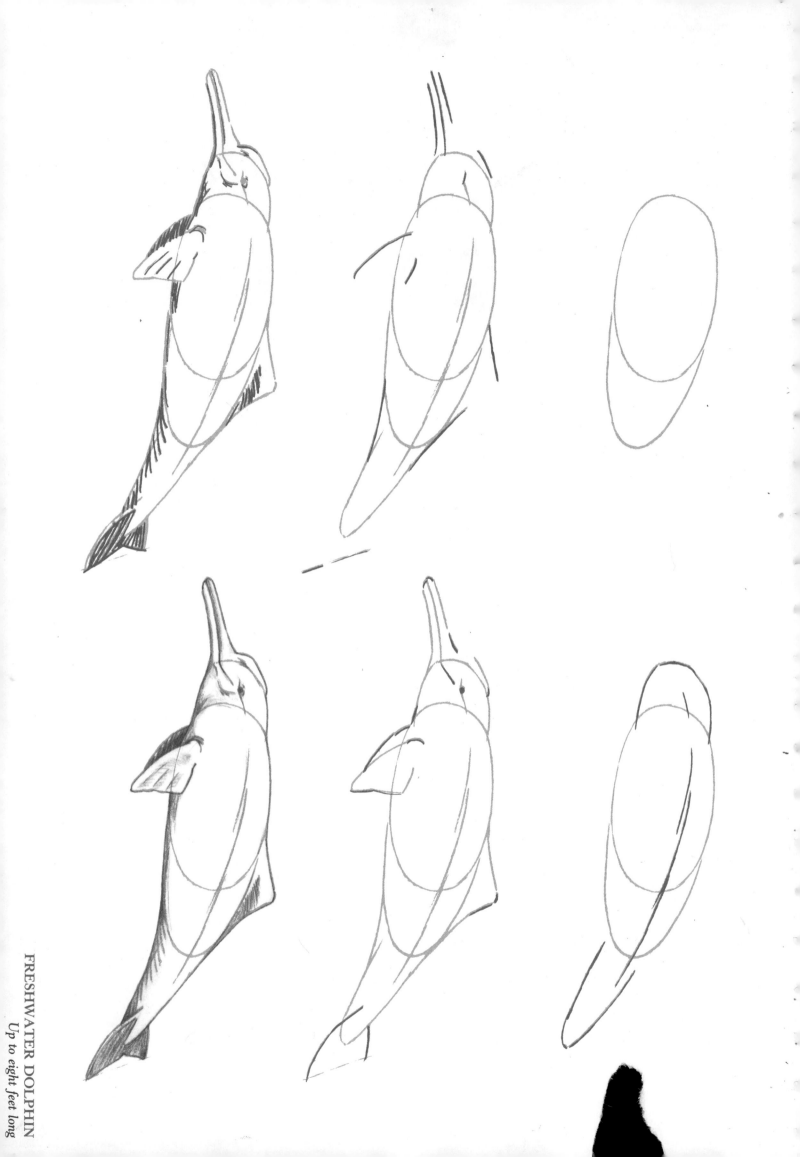

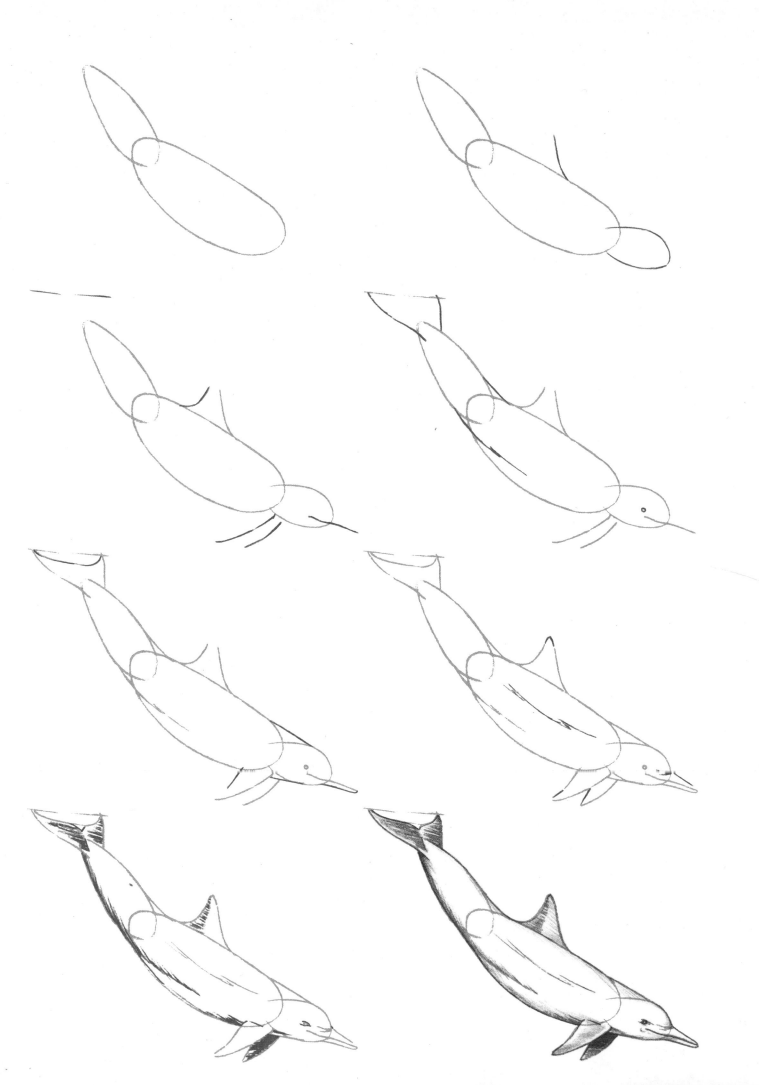

SPINNER DOLPHIN
*Named for its spinning jumps,
this dolphin grows to about six feet long.*

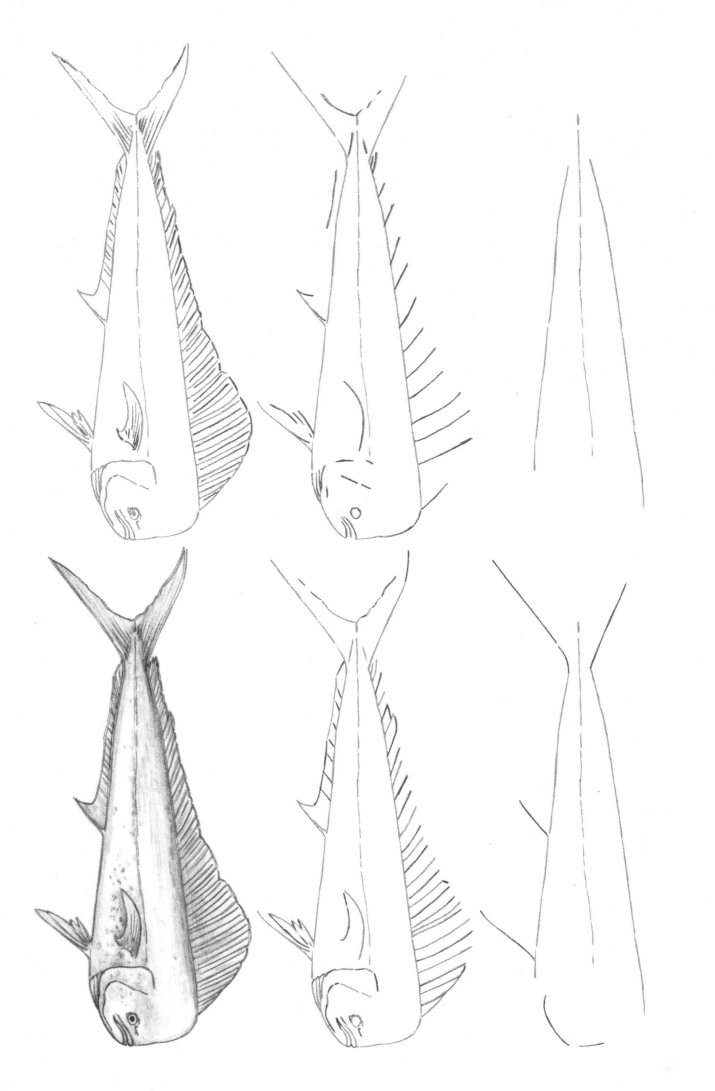

DOLPHIN FISH or **DORADO**
This dolphin is a fish, not a mammal.

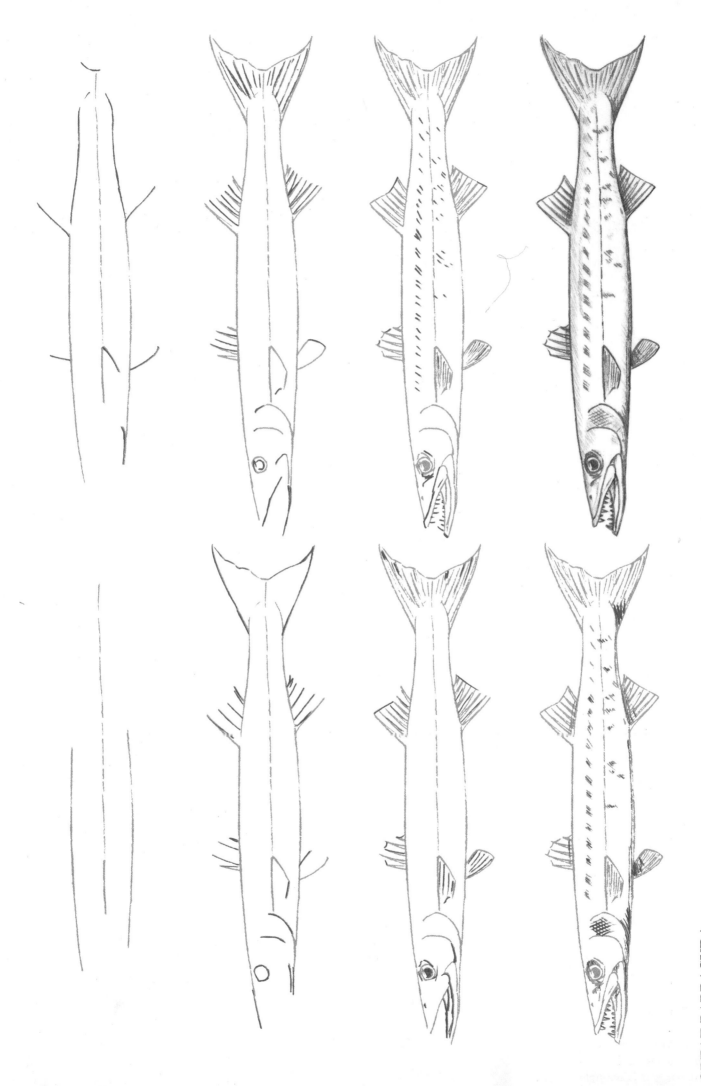

GREAT BARRACUDA

Up to ten feet long, this fish is capable of swimming more than twenty-five miles per hour.

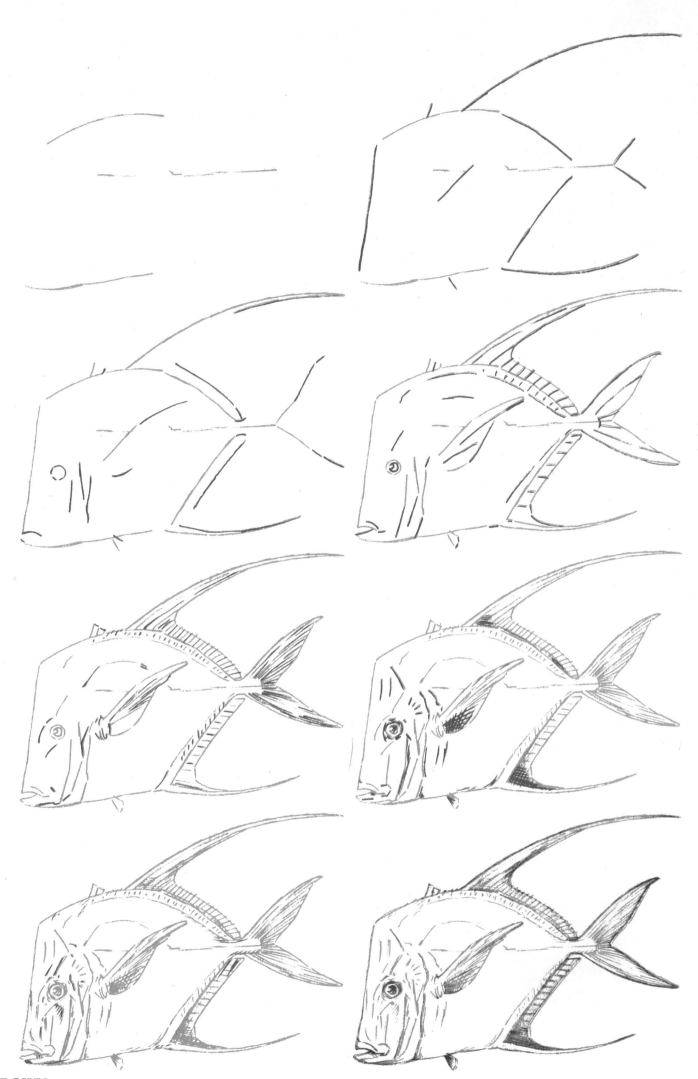

LOOK DOWN
*Up to nine inches long,
the look down is a fierce fighting fish.*

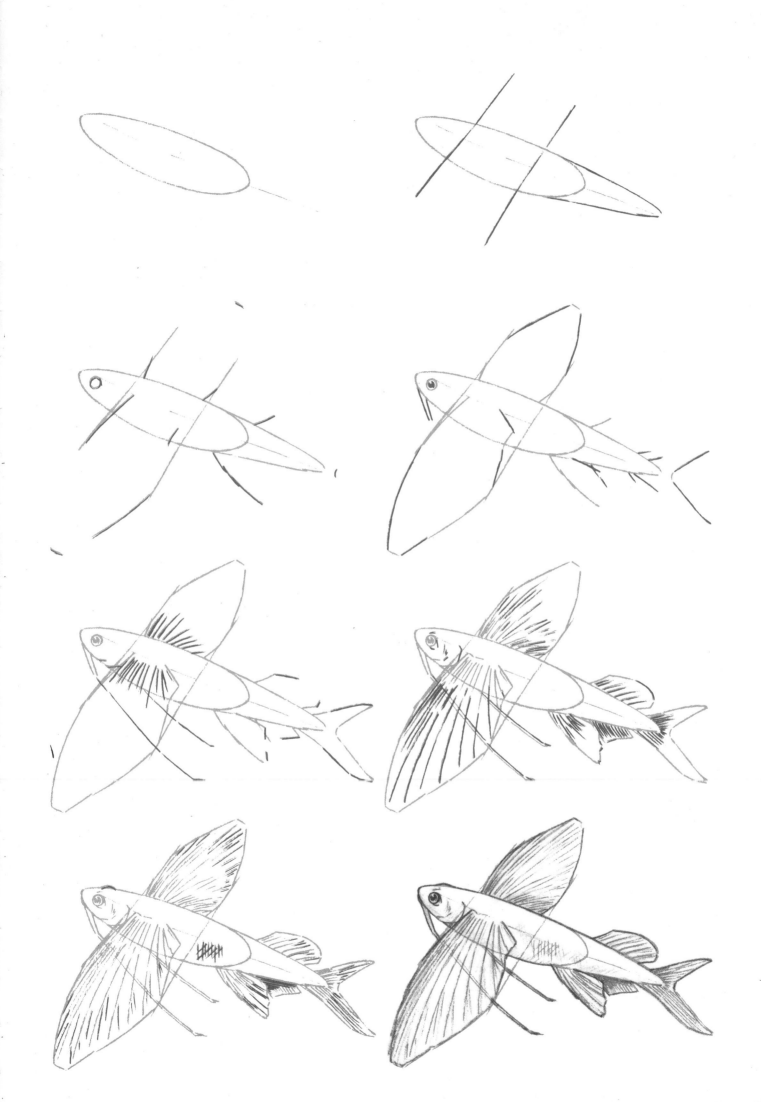

MARGINED FLYING FISH
Up to twelve inches long

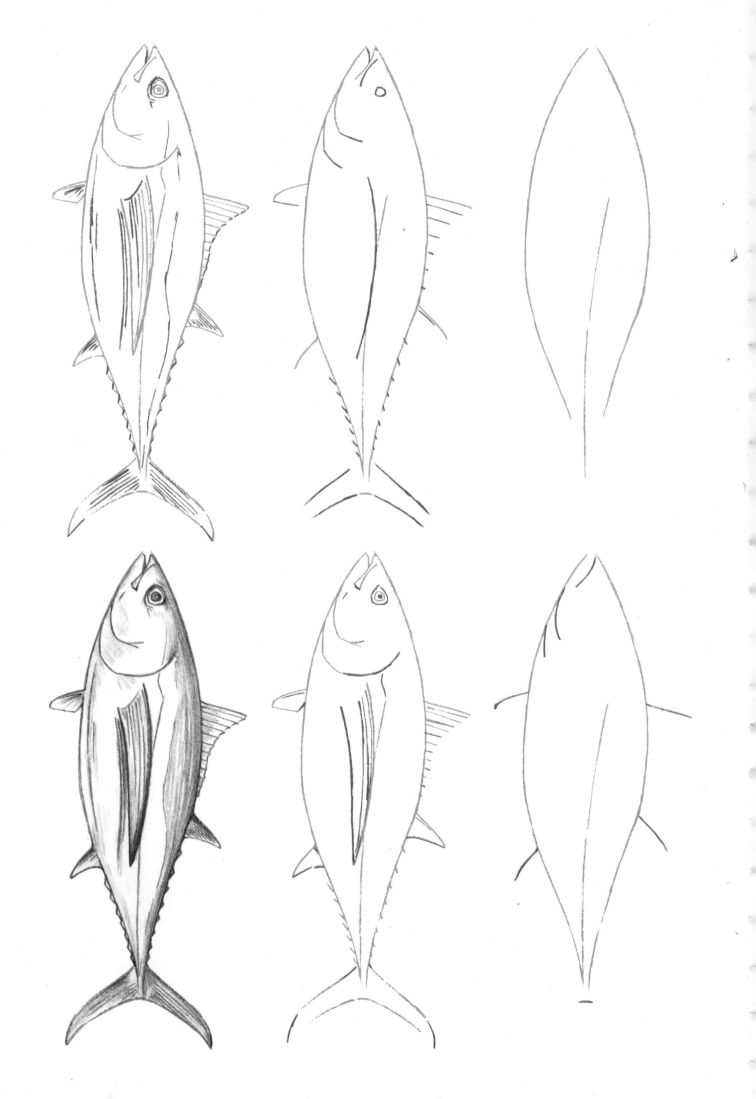

ALBACORE (LONGFIN) TUNA
Up to thirteen feet long

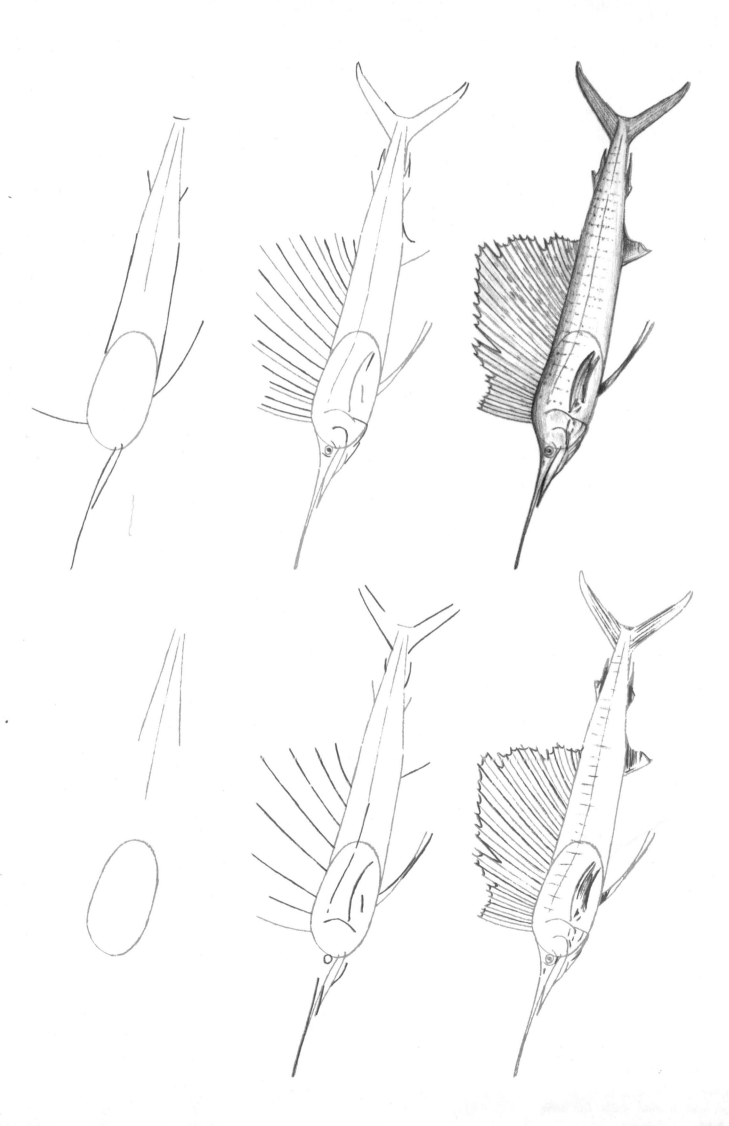

SAILFISH
Up to twelve feet long

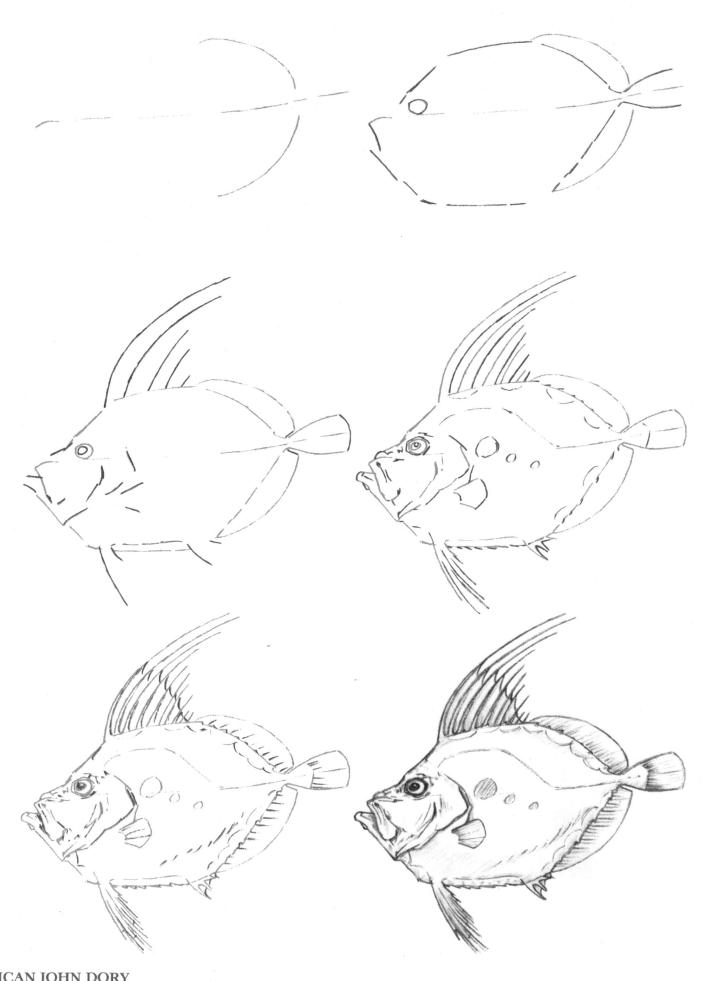

AMERICAN JOHN DORY
Up to twenty-four inches long,
this fish lives in water 1,200 feet deep.

COMMON CUTTLEFISH
Up to twelve inches long

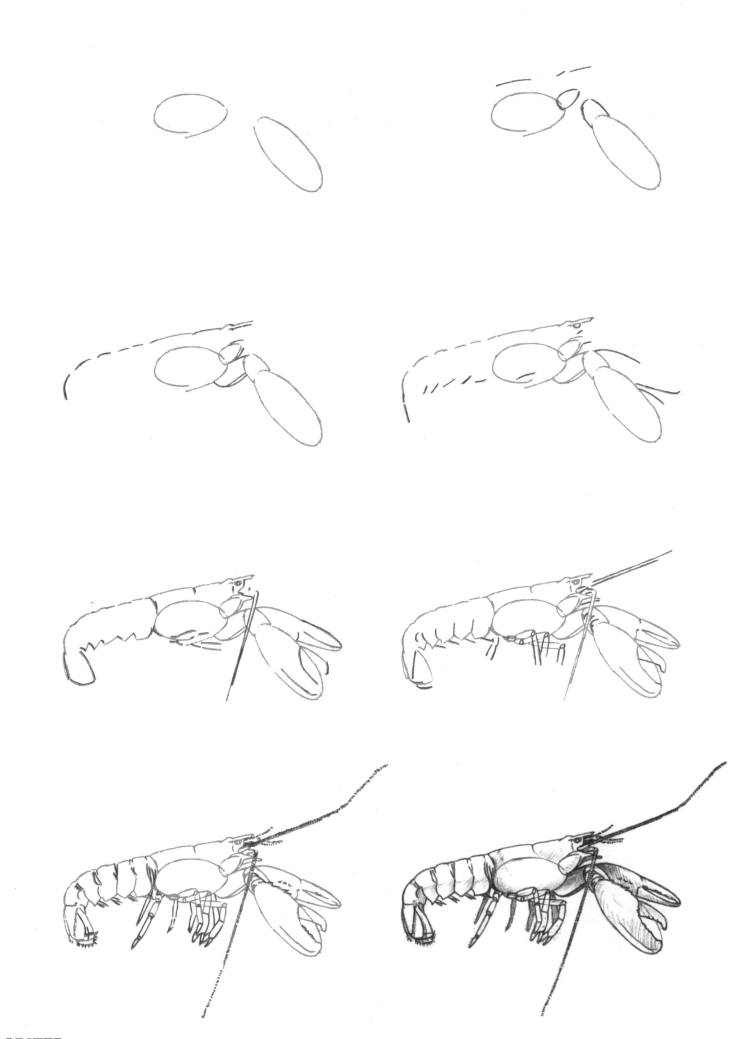

LOBSTER
*Classified as a **Crustacean**,*
lobsters can weigh up to five pounds.

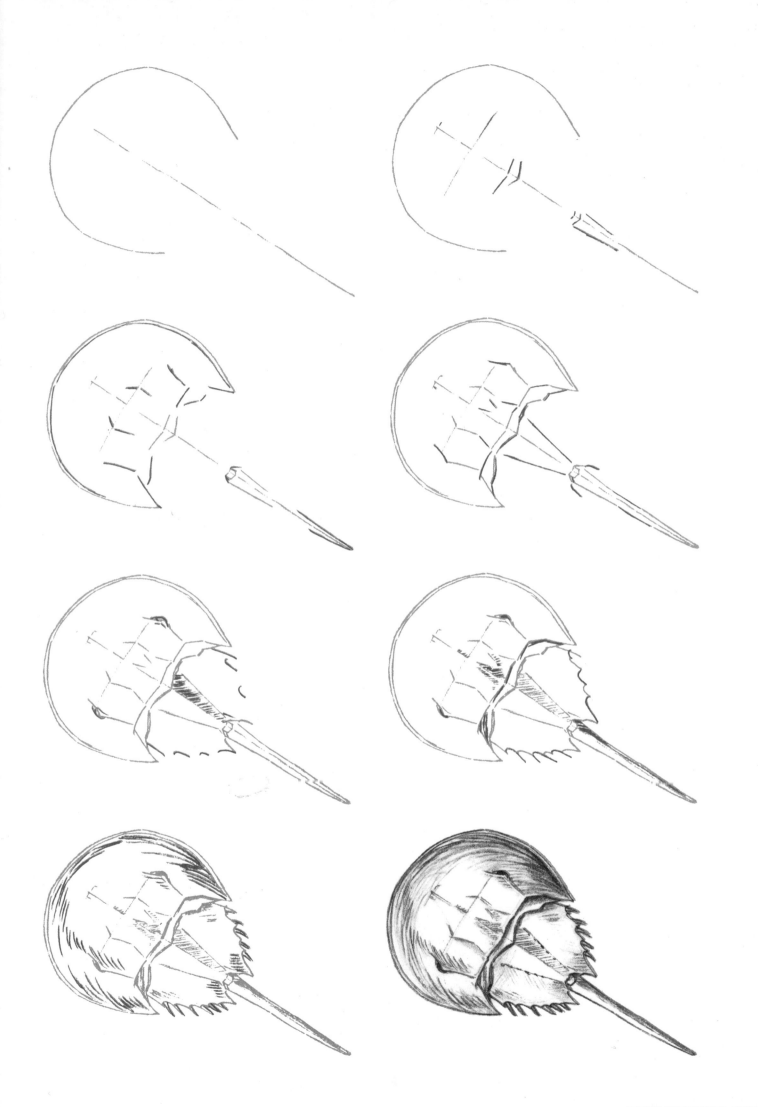

HORSESHOE CRAB
Up to three feet long

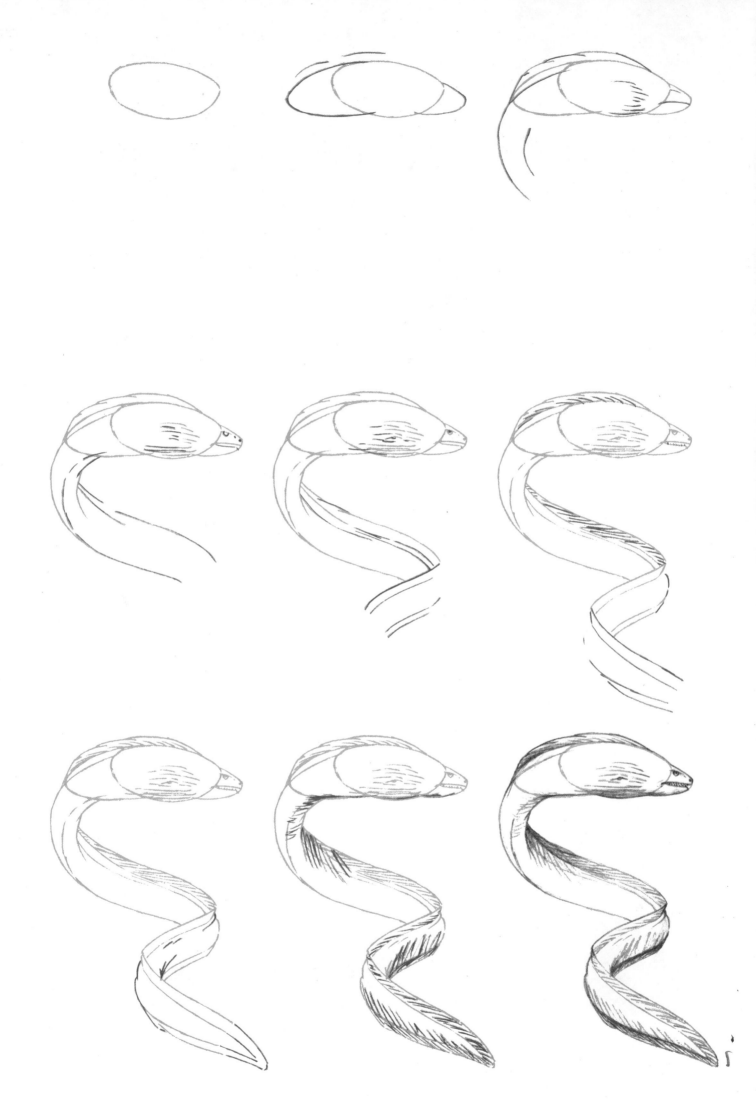

MORAY EEL
Up to six feet long

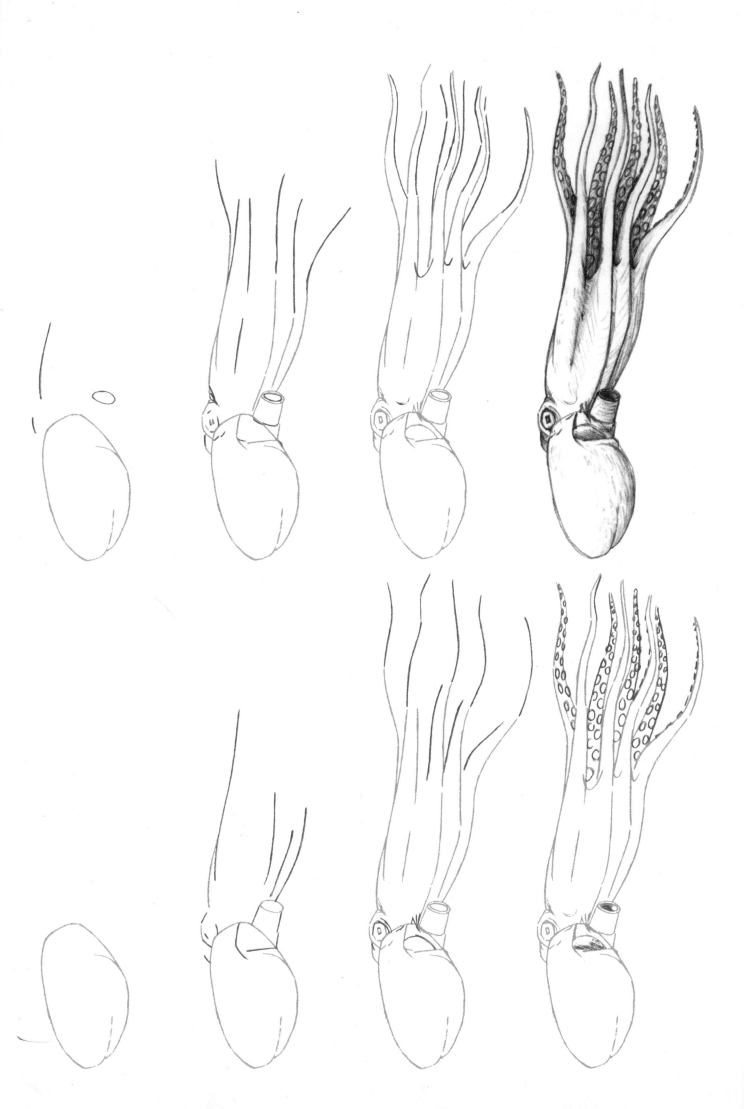

COMMON OCTOPUS
Up to three feet long

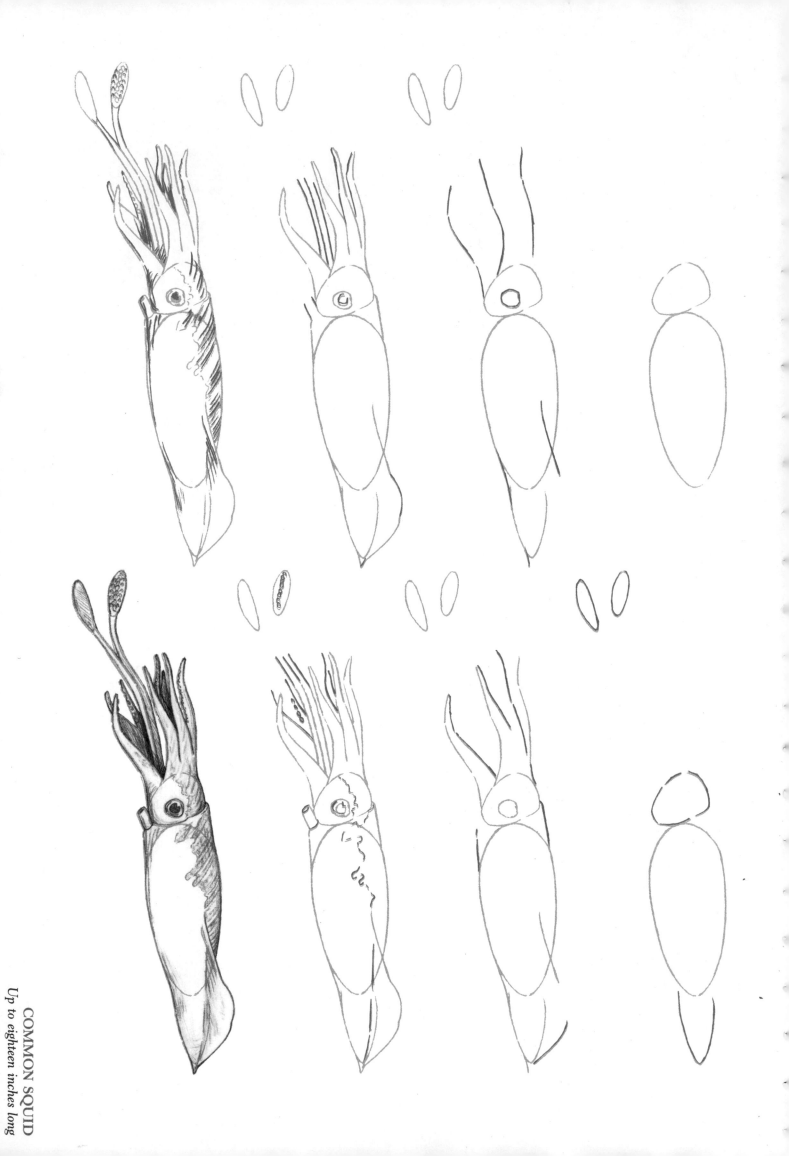

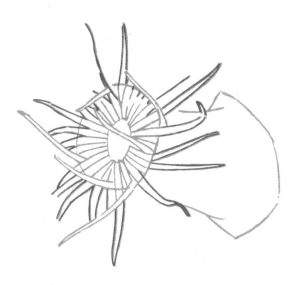

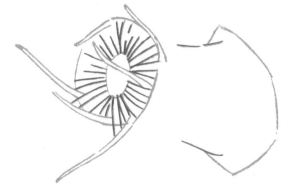

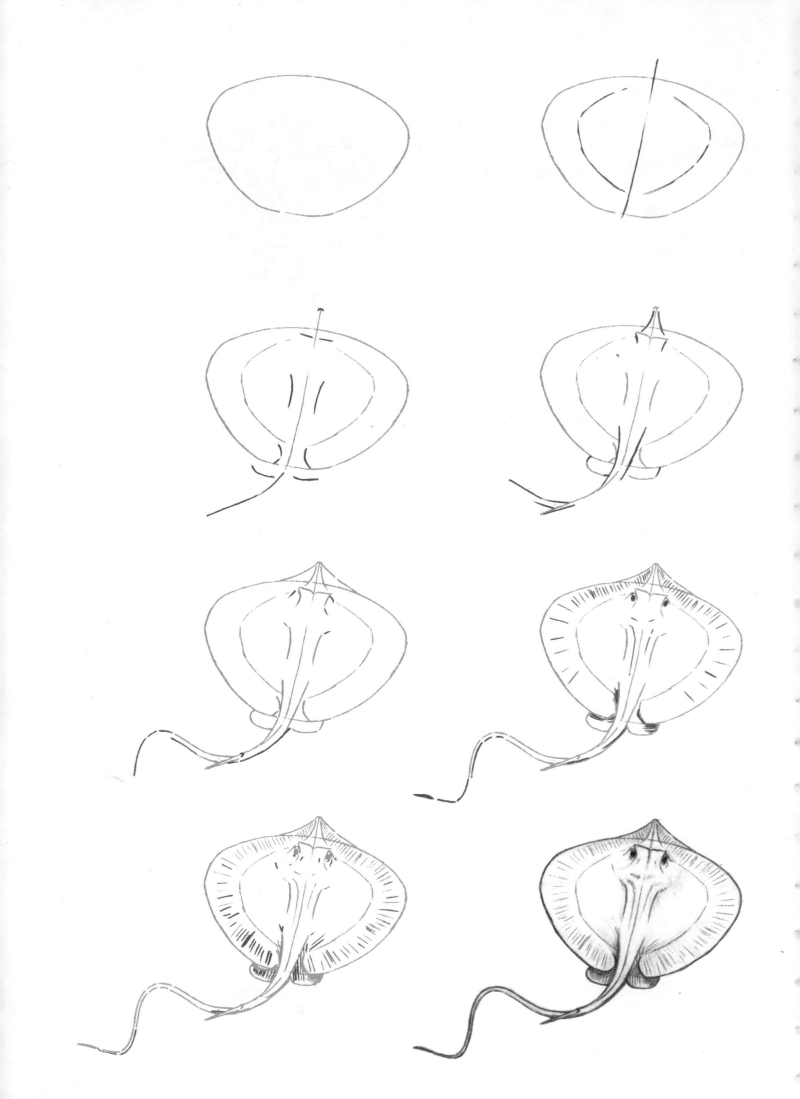

ATLANTIC STINGRAY
Up to seven feet long

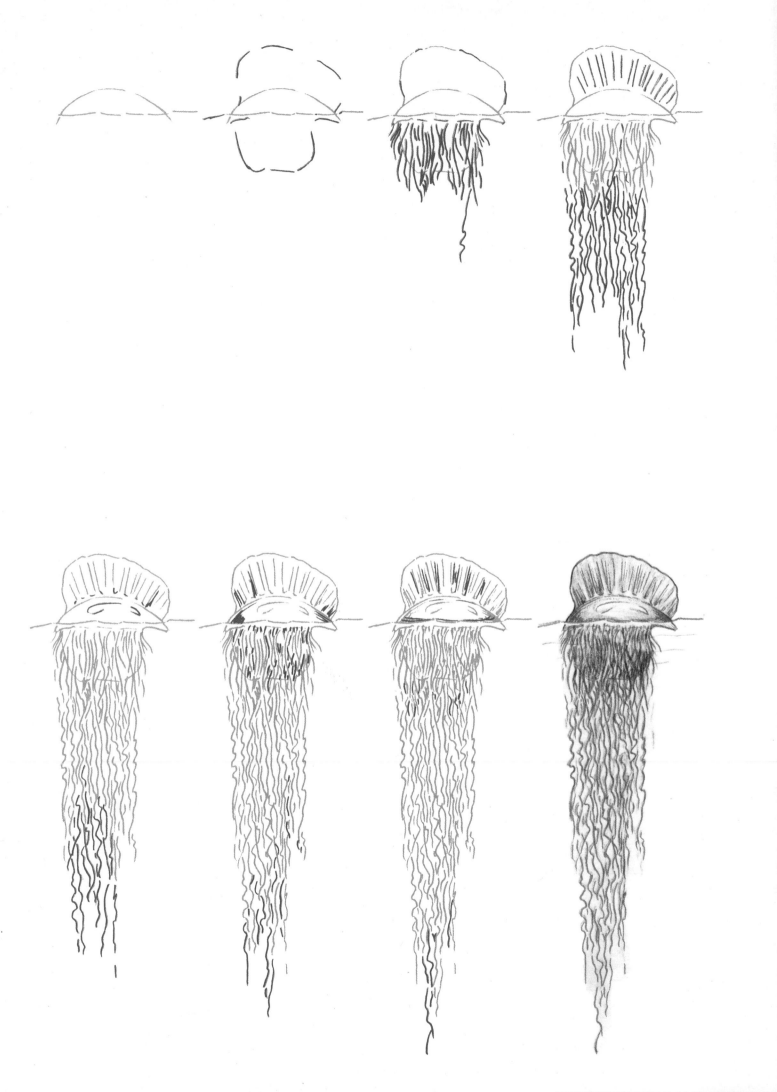

PORTUGUESE MAN-OF-WAR
Tentacles up to fifty feet long

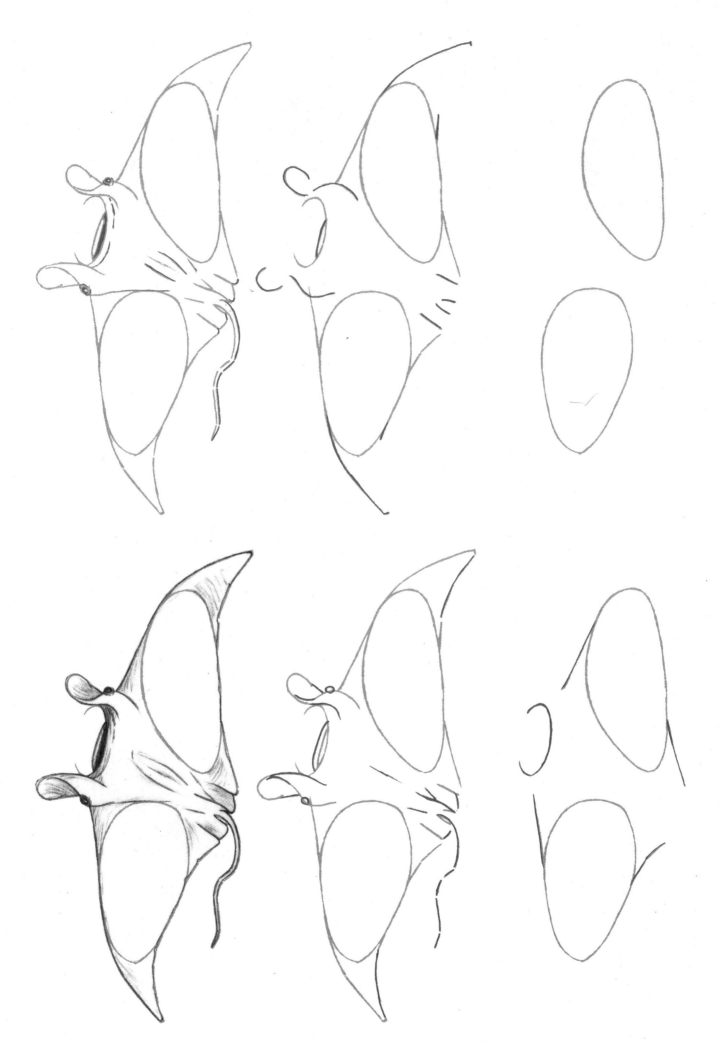

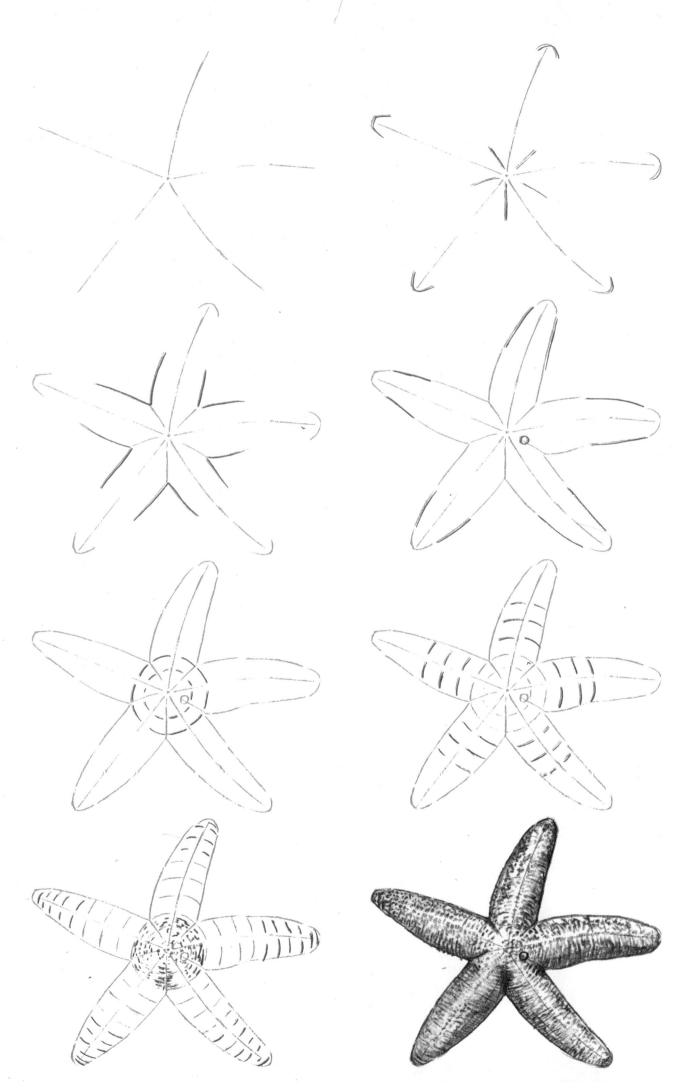

STARFISH

If the Starfish loses an arm, it grows back. Additionally, the arm that falls off will eventually become another Starfish.

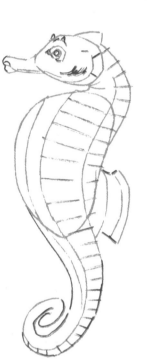
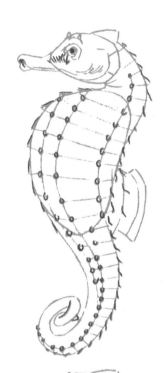
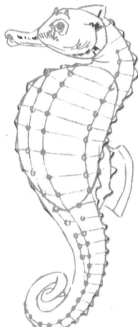
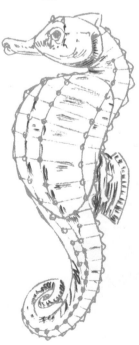

COMMON SEAHORSE (FEMALE)
Unlike other sea creatures, the seahorse
swims upright. It grows up to eight inches long.

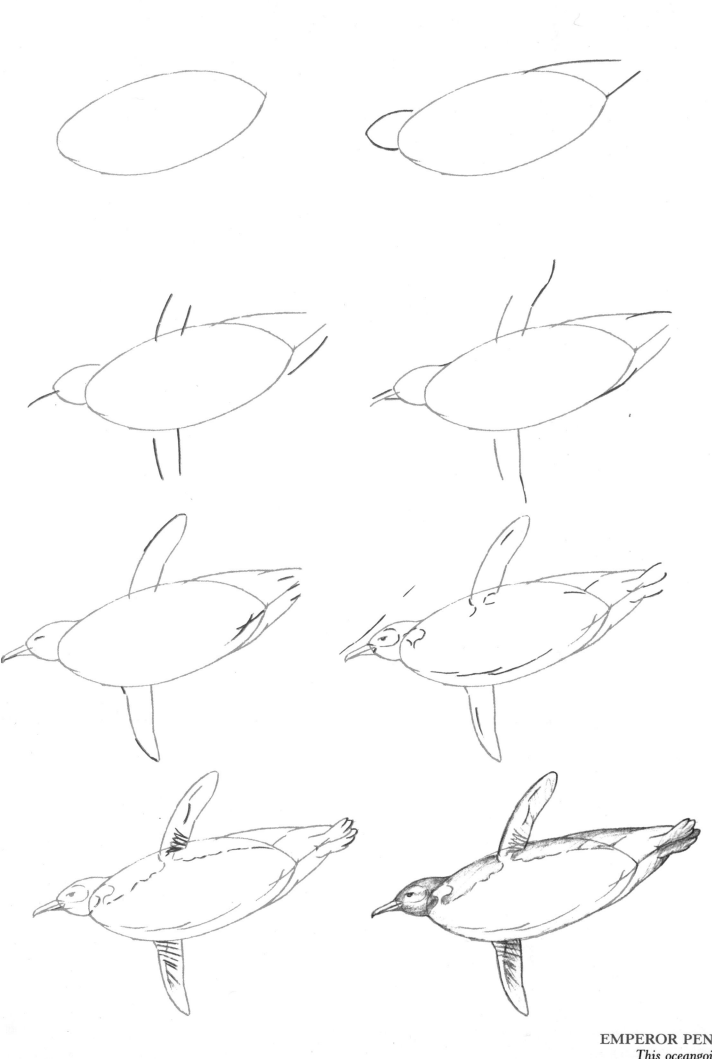

EMPEROR PENGUIN
This oceangoing bird grows up to four feet long.

GREEN TURTLE

*This sea turtle is a reptile
weighing up to five-hundred pounds.*

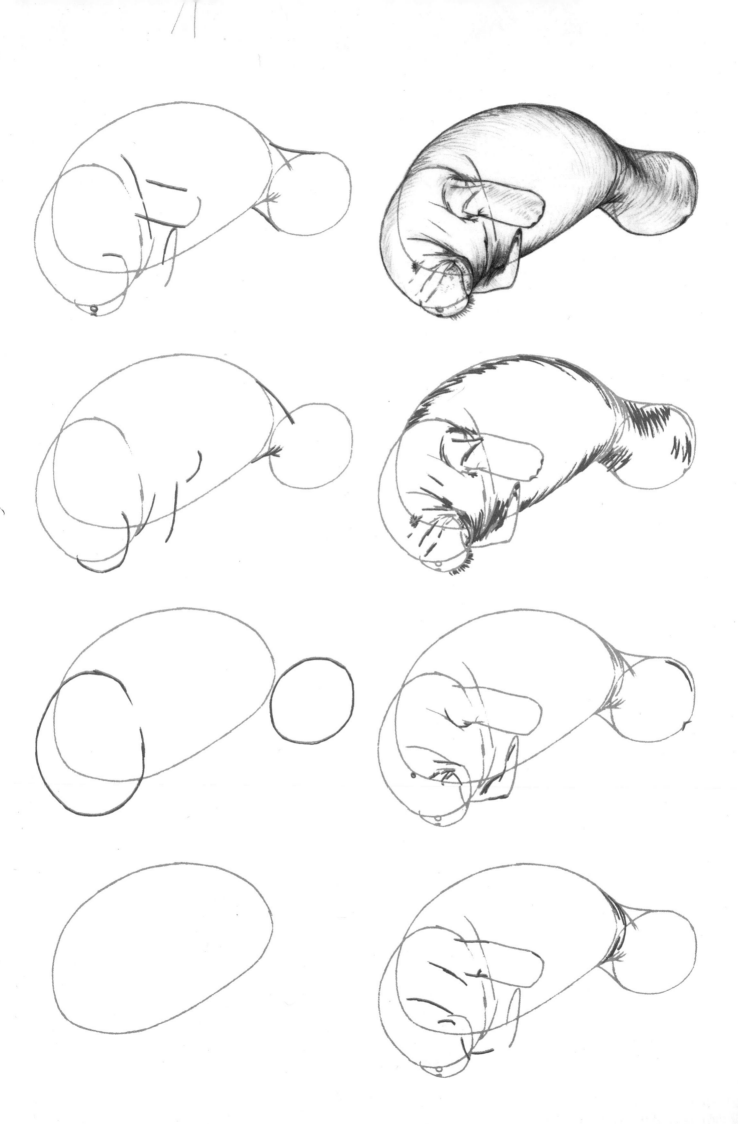

MANATEE
Up to twelve feet long

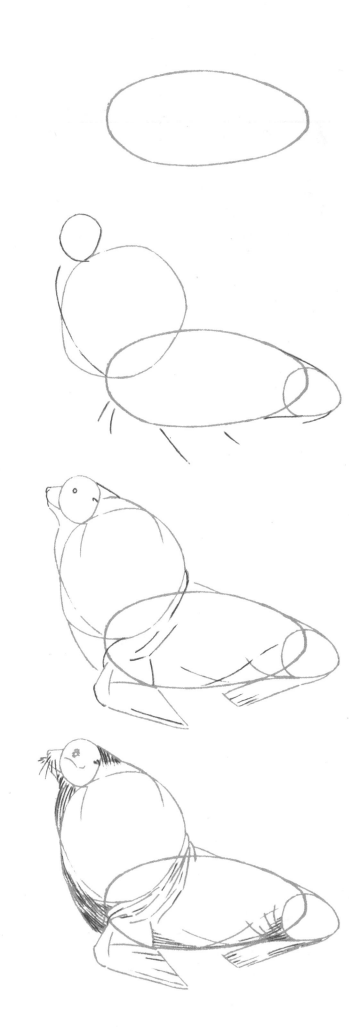
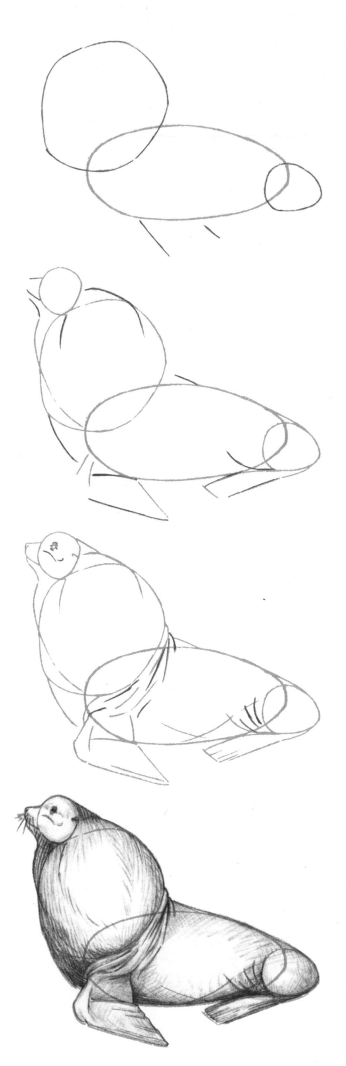

STELLAR SEA LION
This is the largest of the sea lions,
with the male weighing in at around one ton.

WALRUS
*All walruses have tusks and live
only in the Arctic (North Pole) waters.*

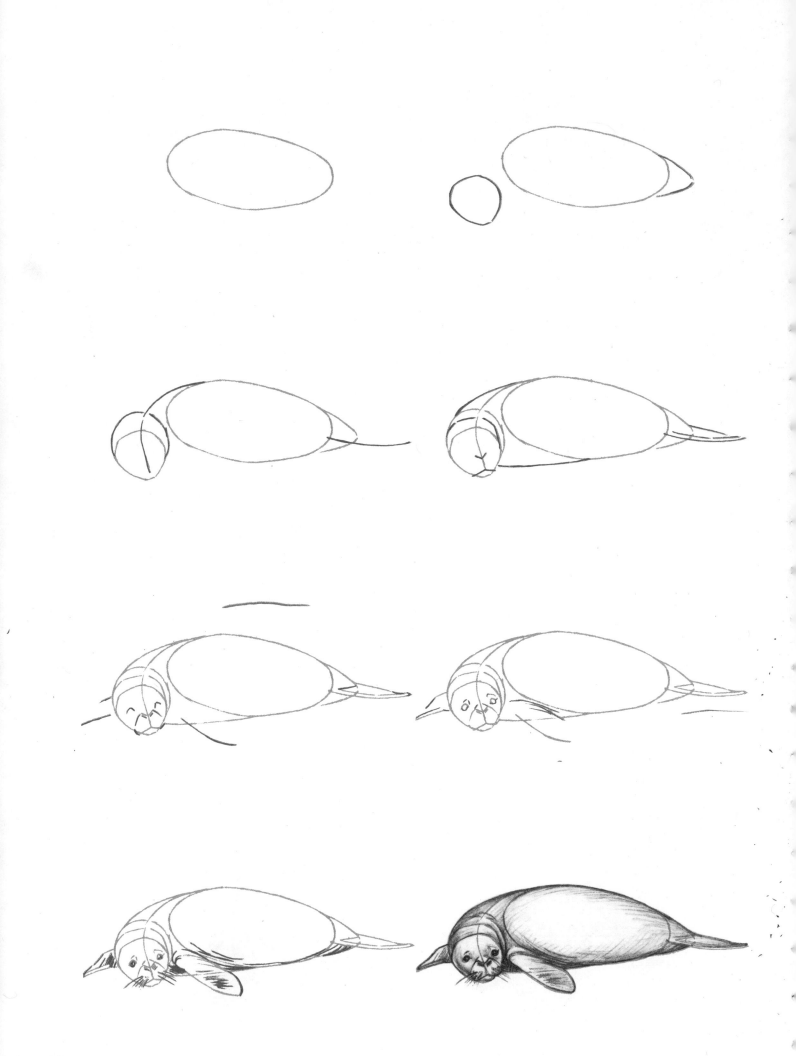

CARIBBEAN MONK SEAL
Unlike the sea lion, the seal has no ears.
It lives in water close to land.

LEE J. AMES joined the Doubleday list in 1962, and since that time his popular drawing books have sold close to one and a half million copies. Utilizing a unique, step-by-step method to guide the young artist's hand, Ames's "Draw 50" books have inspired the creativity of countless children (and adults).

His artistic experience runs the gamut from working at Walt Disney Studios in the days when *Fantasia* and *Pinocchio* were created to teaching at New York City's School of Visual Arts to running his own advertising agency. In addition, he has illustrated over 150 books, from preschool picture books to postgraduate texts.

When not working in his studio, Lee can be found on the tennis courts in Long Island, New York, where he currently lives with his wife, Jocelyn.

Native Long Islander **WARREN BUDD** holds a Bachelor's Degree in Fine Arts from Southhampton College. Primarily a natural science artist, he has been illustrating books for the past eight years. He and his wife, Christine, live in Long Island with their two children—Bryan and Drew.